Continuum Research Methods

Research Questions

Continuum Research Methods Series

Series Editor: Richard Andrews

Judith Bennett: *Evaluation Methods in Research*
Andrew Burn and David Parker: *Analysing Media Texts*
Patrick Costello: *Action Research*
Ian Gregory: *Ethics in Research*
Jill Jameson and Yvonne Hillier: *Researching
    Post-compulsory Education*
Lia Litosseliti: *Using Focus Groups in Research*
Carole Torgerson: *Systematic Reviews*

Real World Research Series

Series Editor: Bill Gillham

Bill Gillham: *Case Study in Research Methods*
Bill Gillham: *Developing a Questionnaire*
Bill Gillham: *The Research Interview*

Research Questions

Richard Andrews

continuum
LONDON • NEW YORK

Continuum

The Tower Building
11 York Road
London SE1 7NX
www.continuumbooks.com

15 East 26th Street
New York
NY 10010

British Library Cataloguing in Publication Data
A catalogue record for this book is available from the British Library.

ISBN: 0-8264-6476-9 (paperback) SMC 610.72 AND

Library of Congress Cataloging-in-Publication Data
A catalogue record of this book has been applied for.

Typeset by Photoprint, Torquay, Devon
Printed and bound in Great Britain by MPG Books, Bodmin, Cornwall

Contents

Dedication

To my research students: past, present and future

Series Editor's Introduction

The *Continuum Research Methods* series aims to provide undergraduate, Masters and research students with accessible and authoritative guides to particular aspects of research methodology. Each title looks specifically at one topic and gives it in-depth treatment, very much in the tradition of the *Rediguide* series of the 1960s and 1970s.

Such an approach allows students to choose the books that are most appropriate to their own projects, whether they are working on a short dissertation, a medium-length work (15–40000 words) or a fully-fledged thesis at MPhil or PhD level. Each title includes examples of students' work, clear explication of the principles and practices involved, and summaries of how best to check that your research is on course.

In due course, individual titles will be combined into larger books and, subsequently, into encyclopaedic works for reference.

The series will also be of use to researchers designing funded projects, and to supervisors who wish to recommend in-depth help to their research students.

Richard Andrews

Acknowledgements

I wish to acknowledge, with thanks, the work of research students cited and quoted in this book: Amna al-Suwaidi, Nancy Cao, Anne Dean, Val Featherstone, Gan Li, David Howes, Sabrina Huang, Winnie Hui, Gwen Kwok, Joanna Lee, Annah Levinovic-Healy, Makie Mori, Teadira Pérez, Erna Puri, Chandra Bhusan Sharma, Daniel Tabor, Evanthia Tsaliki, Qing Yang, Angela Yannicopoulou and You Jin. Their work, and that of other students I have supervised or examined, has helped me to develop the ideas presented here. I hope that what I have learnt from them will help future students to design and conduct their research.

1

The Nature of Questions

In an excellent short book on the nature of questions (Mitchell, 1992), Sally Mitchell explores the question as a social and linguistic device. While not a study of *research* questions, this work explores important aspects of the question that we need to take into account in asking research questions. The book, in fact, starts with a question:

> Ask yourself: what is it like to be asked a question?
>
> (p. 5)

Although, in designing your research project – whether it be a short dissertation, a thesis, or the main question for a large-scale research project – you will be asking rather than answering the question, it is important to remember what it is like to be on the receiving end. If you use a questionnaire or interview as one of your research methods, your respondents will be on the receiving end. Mitchell continues:

> Are you thinking about who's doing the asking, where, when, how, why? While the results of your reflections may be highly dependent on answers to these supplementary questions, it is perhaps possible to arrive at a general conclusion: being asked a question certainly feels like being challenged or tested in some way. Most of us feel pressure to answer: it is only politicians who have

mastered the skill of evading questions without an apology or a blush.

(Ibid.)

Questions, then, are context-related and usually the power rests with the questioner.

As a researcher, you are in a powerful position because you are framing and controlling the study. Although you have a responsibility to be sensitive to the context within which you are working, and although you will trial and test your methodology to make sure it is appropriate to the task in hand you still hold the power as to how the research will be conducted and what the main question will be. As you put questions to your respondents, you are partly determining their responses. This is what Mitchell says about asking a question, as opposed to answering it:

> Very often it is to find yourself in a position of exercising control. At a talk, when the speaker has finished speaking, this control is, by convention, handed over to the previously passive listeners. Often the opportunity is only taken up by those who already hold power, the teachers, the experts, the adults.

(Ibid.)

So, you have a degree of control over the research process by posing a question, and then by asking sub-questions to your respondents.

What else does framing your research in terms of a question or questions imply? *Research* questions are not like ordinary questions. They are somewhat inquisitorial in that they expect an answer (not necessarily a reply). A research question must be *answerable*. This means that it is not helpful in research to have a question that is so all-embracing that it would be impossible to answer it within the confines of a research project, however large. For example, a student may aspire to answer a question like

'What is the nature of education?' or 'What is the impact of communication technologies on learning worldwide?', but to answer those satisfactorily within a dissertation, research project or thesis may be beyond the student's resources and, furthermore, impossible in themselves. The implication here is that is not sufficient just to pose questions: they have to be answered – or, at least, answerable.

By 'answerable' I mean that a research question must have the potential for being answered in the project to be undertaken. It may well turn out that the question does not have a clear answer. Such an outcome is acceptable, because at least you have tried to answer it. Your results might be illuminating; they might suggest the question should have been re-framed in some way; your results might be 'negative' in that they don't turn out to be the way you expected or predicted they would turn out. All these possible outcomes are positive in research, because we will know more at the end of the research process that we did at the beginning about the substantial focus or process of the research.

Take the word 'impact' for example. Scientists and social scientists, psychologists and others operating within a largely scientific paradigm feel largely confident that they can measure 'effect' by undertaking a randomized controlled trial. Essentially, such a trial or experiment sets up two groups – a control group and an experimental group – and an intervention is carried out on the experimental group to see if it has any effect. Randomization is simply the best way to ensure that the two samples are as equivalent as possible. Within such a paradigm, it is assumed that x might have a causal effect on y, all other factors or 'variables' being equal or controlled. *Impact*, however, is a broader term than 'effect'. The operation of one phenomenon on another is less tightly – logically,

3

causally – related and might be indirect as well as direct. It is therefore necessary to define what you mean by 'impact'. Does it stand mid-way between the tightly framed and measurable 'effect' on the one hand, and the vaguely felt 'influence' on the other? If so, exactly where does it stand? Some people feel it is synonymous with 'effect'; others don't. Does it imply strategic considerations as well as causal ones? Is it multi-factored rather than the result of a single factor? If so, what methodology and methods might be employed to find an answer to a question of the *impact* of *x* on *y*?

What the foregoing discussion might have revealed is that the *scale* of a question is crucial to the design of the rest of the study. Some questions are bigger than others, and thus require a different approach to answer them. Some of the bigger ones will be unanswerable by research. A very common pattern in research projects and studies is that a broad aim is refined down to a manageable research question in the first stages of the research (and perhaps even during the course of the research itself). This 'refining' is a process of moving from broad, desirable aims of the research to specific working research questions that will determine the shape, direction and progress of the research.

To go back to our earlier example, a question like 'What is the impact of communication technologies on learning worldwide?' is at such a level of generality as to be unanswerable (other than in speculative journalism). Its scale is unmanageable. It could be made more manageable, and thus more researchable, by being reduced to something like 'What is the impact of communication technologies on learning in the UK?' and then further, as in the examples below:

What is the impact of communication technologies on learning in the UK?

What is the impact of laptop computers on learning in the UK?

What is the impact of laptop computers on the learning of 12–14-year-olds in the UK?

What is the impact of laptop computers on the learning of 12–14-year-olds outside school in the UK?

There is still much to be defined: what is meant by 'impact'? What is meant by learning? And is the study intended to cover the whole of the UK or just one of England, Northern Ireland, Scotland or Wales? Each of the questions implies a certain scale of study. You should refine your own question until you are sure that you can manage to answer it within the confines, not only of the length of report or dissertation you'll write, but with regard also to the resources you have at your disposal within the time-frame allocated to the research.

Research questions and rationales

Most questions do not simply form themselves from the air; they derive from contexts, or in response to a situation. Thus knowledge progresses dialogically, or dialectically, in response to an existing state of affairs that is perceived to be incomplete or, at best, a partial solution to contextual needs.

A case in point is language policy in Hong Kong in the post-1997 period. Because of increasing commerce between Hong Kong and mainland China, Mandarin or Putonghua, the Chinese national language, has become an issue for language policy-makers in the special administrative region, where the two most commonly spoken languages are Cantonese (strictly speaking, a dialect of Chinese) and English. The question of whether Putonghua should be used as one of the media of instruction in

Hong Kong schools is a complex one, but a pressing one. With reintegration into China, there are economic as well as political reasons for giving Putonghua a higher profile in the region, not least because of China's entry into the World Trade Organization. Against this background, one student formulated a research question:

Should Putonghua be a medium of instruction in Hong Kong secondary schools?

This is an interesting question in itself, but it is also a very good research question because it is answerable in a number of ways: by talking to young people in the schools, and to headteachers, teacher educators and policy-makers. As a 'should' question, it invites the expression of opinions as empirical data; but as a research question, it also requires a review of the research literature on the topic and of the topical literature in newspapers, magazines and other popular media. At the end of the project, it ought to be possible to arrive at an answer to the question, but at the same time there might be varying degrees of opinion that will be reflected in the responses, and some interesting further lines to pursue. At its simplest, the question invites a 'yes' or 'no' answer (and if the research were conducted via large-scale survey, it would be possible to say 'a majority of those questioned felt that ...'); but at its more complex, the question might be answered with shades of opinion according to particular circumstances. For example, respondents might feel that there are certain conditions and circumstances in which Putonghua is the best medium of instruction, and others where it is not.

The question thus benefits from being framed within a rationale. There is a clear reason for asking the question, and its answer will contribute to public debate as well as adding to the sum of knowledge.

Practical considerations

Cohen *et al.* (2000) helpfully suggest that the scale of research questions depends also on 'orienting decisions' (p. 74), that is, decisions which 'will set the boundaries or parameters of constraints on the research'. The amount of time available for the research, for instance, will affect the kind of question that can be answered, as will the costs available for the conduct of the research. If, as is likely, costs are to be kept to a minimum, then it is sensible not to undertake a national survey involving travel costs. On the other hand, research can be undertaken on a very small budget by using email or face-to-face delivery of questionnaires rather than postage; and by interviewing a relatively small number of respondents so that travel costs – and more importantly, time costs – are kept low. It has to be borne in mind that the transcription of oral interviews is very time-consuming, especially if translation from one language to another is involved.

Thus, for a six-month, a one-year or a three-year project undertaken by a single researcher, the kinds of question that can be asked have to be answerable within the time available. A question like 'What is the effect of the introduction of the National Literacy Strategy on primary school children in England?' would be answerable by a large-scale evaluation involving a team of researchers over a period of a few years. It would not be wise for a single researcher to attempt to answer such a question in a year or even three years. A related, but more manageable, question for a single researcher might be 'What curriculum changes have been brought about by the introduction of the National Literacy Strategy to primary schools in [a particular small town]?' or 'What do teachers think about the National Literacy Strategy and its impact on the primary curriculum in schools in [a particular rural area]?'.

Note that constraints of time and resource have a tendency to affect the paradigm within which the research operates. Small-scale studies rarely address questions of 'effect' in education research because such questions require a randomized controlled trial (a control group and an experimental group with randomized sampling in each case) for maximum validity and reliability although it is possible to undertake small-scale randomized controlled trials (RCTs). 'Effect' questions, furthermore, sit within a scientific paradigm where it is assumed the effect of an 'intervention' can be measured on a state of affairs. In a more humanistic paradigm, research tends to ask questions about attitude or value; about the nature of problems; and about the state of play in a situation. Such a tendency does not mean you have to follow it: it is possible to set up a controlled trial or experiment within, say, a year's study; just as longer and larger-scale projects can ask evaluative questions. Readers interested in the different paradigms in education and social science research are referred to first part of Scott and Usher's *Researching Education* (1999).

There is further advice on the way orienting questions can help determine the nature of research questions in Cohen *et al.* (2000, pp. 83–5). One major difference between the present book's approach and that of Cohen *et al.* is that the latter consistently refer to 'research questions', whereas the present book draws what it sees as a crucial distinction between a main research question and subsidiary questions.

2

How Questions Emerge from Topic Areas or 'Problems'

Research questions can take time to develop. While in many ways they are the starting point for the focused research, they can take weeks or months to develop. In some fields and on some projects, the whole aim might be, over several years, to work towards a research question!

Let us assume that you want to get to your research question within weeks or months. There are two ways to go about the task. One is to work hard and fast, early in the project, to generate and refine your research question. The other is to let the research question emerge from the literature review.

In the first half of 2001, I co-ordinated a project team which was trying to generate a research question in the area of information communication technology (ICT) and literacy learning. We had agreed that this was the broad area in which we wanted to undertake a systematic literature review, but we also knew that the two fields were so large in themselves that the project would be unmanageable if we didn't formulate the research question sharply enough.

Our first step was partly determined by the quasi-scientific world of the systematic review (a literature review which attempts, systematically, to cover a wide range of the literature in as unbiased a way as possible).

9

We were working within a paradigm which expected to find causal relations between different phenomena. In our case, the first move was to determine that we were interested in the effect or impact or influence of ICT on literacy learning. Initially, we were hoping to maintain a two-way relationship between ICT and literacy learning, i.e. what is the influence of ICT on literacy learning and in turn, what is the influence of literacy learning on ICT? We understood at the time – and were later to understand more fully – that the relationship between ICT and literacy learning is symbiotic, and that a one-way causal relationship would only paint part of the picture in this field. Nevertheless, we decided, on the advice of teachers and researchers, to stick to one aspect of the symbiotic relationship: what is the influence/effect/impact of ICT on literacy learning?

As soon as you are beginning to focus on influence or impact or effect, you need to decide how sharp that focus will be – or, more accurately, how tight the aperture will be of your study. *Influence* suggests a wide aperture; *impact* a smaller one; and *effect* the tightest of the three. Because our attention was in a field – education and learning – with a large number of variables and factors at play, we wanted to keep the aperture open a little more widely that would have been suggested by the use of 'effect', and so we decided on 'impact'. Here's how we justified that decision:

> We have chosen 'impact' rather than 'effect' as we wish to determine the broader aspects of the influence of ICT on learning in English (and vice versa) rather than merely attempt to measure effect. The term 'impact' allows us to examine strategies and processes as well as outcomes; we use it to include 'effect' but also to refer to wider (not necessarily causal) influences, e.g. on curriculum or policy.

To choose 'effect' would have meant that we would need

a very different kind of study. To measure effect it is almost always necessary to set up a control group and experimental group. The effect of an intervention is measured in the experimental group by comparing it with the effect (or lack of it) in the control group. The aim of the experiment is to determine the effect an intervention has; and its reliability is a measure of whether the same effect would have been observed if the experiment had been undertaken with another group of equally randomized subjects or respondents.

Our choice of 'impact' rather than 'effect' was critical in our study, because it allowed us to look at a wider range of study types than the randomized controlled trial. In other words, we were able to look at most study types.

So far, then, the research question had reached the state of 'What is the impact of ICT on literacy learning?'.

Before we go on to delimit and contain the question further, let us pause and consider what we mean by two key terms in the question: *ICT* and *literacy*. Most research projects define key terms so that it is clear what is meant, in particular, by these terms in the course of the research and in its reporting. Our project was no exception:

> ICT stands for 'information and communication technol-ogies'. In the proposed systematic review, we limit our-selves to networked technologies with a multimodal interface, i.e. networked and stand-alone computers, mobile phones with the capacity for a range of types of communication, and other technologies which allow multimodal and interactive communication. In terms of the use of ICT in subject English (and other subjects in the curriculum), the National Curriculum for England suggests that '. . . pupils should be given opportunities to apply and develop their ICT capability through the use of ICT tools to support their learning' and they 'should be given opportunities to support their work by being taught

11

to (a) find out things from a variety of sources, selecting and synthesizing information to meet needs and developing an ability to question its accuracy, bias and plausibility, (b) develop their ideas using ICT tools to amend and refine their work and enhance its quality and accuracy, (c) exchange and share information, both directly and through electronic media and (d) review, modify and evaluate their work, reflecting critically on its quality, as it progresses' (DfEE/QCA, 1999 (English) p. 52).

We have chosen 'literacy' for a number of reasons: first, to delimit the field of enquiry to reading and writing; second, to distinguish the learning literacy from the subject English as taught in the National Curriculum for England [the National Curriculum was established in England and Wales in the early 1990s and is statutory for the 5–16 year old curriculum in state schools]; third, because as a term (especially in its pluralistic sense of 'literacies') it is both narrowly definable and open to wider interpretation; and fourth, because it allows us to review research that takes place outside formal education, e.g. in homes and other communities in which young people operate. In the proposed study, we will focus on reading and writing (in the broadest senses of those terms). Such delimiting of the focus of our review does not mean that the results of the review will not be relevant to the teaching of literacy in other countries; nor that we will limit ourselves to research undertaken in England. On the contrary, our net is spread wide.

These initial discussions of definitions were refined into shorter, working definitions for the purposes of the research process:

ICT stands for 'information and communication technologies', networked technologies with a multimodal interface, ie. networked and stand-alone computers, mobile phones with the capacity for a range of types of communication, and other technologies which allow multimodal and interactive communication.

'Literacy' can be defined narrowly, as the ability to understand and create written language. But firstly, the scope can be expanded so that written language becomes written language and graphical or pictorial representation. Secondly, the skill can be treated as social, rather than psychological; in this view literacy is the ability to operate a series of social or cultural representations. Since sets of expectations and norms differ depending on the situation, the social view of literacy entails a number of different 'literacies'.

The point here is that definitions themselves might have to be refined during the course of determining the research question.

At this point, we are not much further on in the shaping of the research question, but we do have a very sharp sense of what the core of the research question means: 'What is the impact of ICT on literacy learning?'

You will have noticed that the word 'learning' is still undefined. This is because we have taken 'literacy learning' as a compound concept. However, the concept needs further definition. We achieved such refinement by adding elements to the research question. First, we added the fact that we were limiting the study to literacy learning *in English* – and by 'English', we meant the English language as spoken, listened to, read and written and as part of multimodal communication either as a mother tongue or as an additional language. Our proposal or protocol read as follows:

> By 'English-speaking countries' we mean any country or state which uses English as a first language or second/third language, especially where in the latter case English is not only the language of research publication, but also a language taught in the curriculum between 5 and 16, e.g. Hong Kong, Singapore

Essentially, then, we were going to look at what is commonly known as 'English as a Second Language (ESL)' or 'English as an Additional Language (EAL)' rather than at 'English as a Foreign Language (EFL)'.

Our research question now looked like this 'What is the impact of ICT on literacy learning in English?'. We

13

had thought of further defining 'English' by delimiting it to the subject English as taught in the National Curriculum for England and Wales. However, the use of 'English' in that context clashed with our broader definitions of 'literacies', especially with regard to multimodal and visual (still and moving image) literacies, and thus was thought to be unsuitable; furthermore, a definition of 'English' based on curricula in England and Wales would not have suited the international range of reference we had in mind.

Finally, we wished to limit the particular study to the compulsory years of schooling in most countries, so the final research question became 'What is the impact of ICT on literacy learning in English, 5–16?'.

The advantage of such a sharply honed question is that it helps in defining the scope of the literature review, as well as providing an answerable question that will determine the structure and development of the research project. Our systematic review required us to go one stage further, and develop inclusion criteria to determine the direction, nature and quality of the literature review. To be included in our review, studies would have to:

> be a systematic review, an intervention (outcome or process evaluation) or a non-intervention;
> have as their main focus ICT applications to literacy development;
> focus on literacy learning and teaching in schools and/ or homes;
> be about the impact of ICT on literacy development;
> be published in English, in the period 1990–2001;
> look at literacy and ICT in English-speaking countries;
> be a completed study;
> be studies whose participants/study population includes children at ages 5–16;
> not be opinion pieces.

You can see from the inclusion criteria that we have added further constraints: on time (1990–2001), that the work be published in English, be completed studies and not be opinion pieces. Even with such meticulous refining of the research question, our searches of a number of electronic databases and hand-searches of a number of journals in the field revealed nearly 2000 articles, chapters and books: more than enough, as an initial trawl, for a Masters or Doctoral thesis.

During the course of the study, we discovered that to answer the research question, 'What is the impact of ICT on literacy learning in English, 5–16?' involved a number of subsidiary questions. For example, ICT's impact on literacy can be manifested in word-processing and composition, via networked technologies (email, the Internet), on reading, on dyslexia and so on. In practical terms, we decided to complete one of these subsidiary areas before embarking on the answering of the overarching research question. In this example, then, a subsidiary question, 'What is the impact of *networked* ICT on literacy learning in English, 5–16?' became a contributory research question – a contribution to answering the overall question with which we embarked on the research.

Research questions emerging from a literature review

Rather than start a project with the generation and development of a research question, an alternative approach is to let the question(s) emerge from a literature review. In such an approach, the thesis usually starts with the identification of a nexus of issues, which in turn may have emerged in public debate, through the media and/or in the mind of the researcher. For example, in Tabor (2001) the conventional 'Introduction' chapter is replaced with an introductory chapter that explores such a nexus of issues. This first, introductory chapter, entitled

15

'Transition, continuity and progression' (three key terms in the research project) is structured as follows:

It is possible to tell from the structure of the chapter and length of each section that this chapter is contextual; it is an overture to the thesis itself, identifying the main issues and problems which the research will address. The section on 'Transition, continuity and progression' and the sub-section on 'The dip in pupils' achievements' are the longest, indicating where the main issues lie. The section, 'Recent research on transition, continuity and progression', even though it is eighteen pages in length, does not pretend to be a full-scale literature review on the topics – that comes in a second, much longer chapter.

The second chapter addresses these issues in more depth. There is extensive discussion of models of writing development; notions of progression and continuity in the National Curriculum; teachers' and pupils' attitudes to writing at the transition; and a section on boys and English. As the researcher puts it, 'The main issue emerging from the literature review in chapters 1 and 2 is that there is a problem about writing at transition, i.e. between primary and secondary schools'. Interestingly, the sub-issue of writing at the transition did not emerge centrally in the first chapter, which focused on progression, continuity and transition from primary to secondary school *in general*. During the process of writing the literature review – or at least, in the course of the second chapter – the specific issue centres on *writing*. Through repeated mention in the research literature and through the researcher's own predilection for research on the subject of English, writing at the transition becomes the principal focus. It has the advantage of being more contained a topic that transition in general; and it gives rise to the research questions. In the case of this research project, we are a third of the way through the thesis as a whole. The rest of the thesis is structured to answer those questions.

The actual research questions are discussed in detail in a subsequent chapter of the present book. Suffice it to say, at this point, that the focus on writing acts enables the research to undertake a feasible study that will shed light on the broader question of transition in general. The fourth and most general of the research questions is 'What do the answers to the [previous three questions on writing] tell us about transition and progression as pupils move from primary to secondary school?'.

There are advantages and disadvantages in arriving at research questions through a literature review. The advantages are that the question(s) will be well-grounded in existing research (assuming the literature review is a good one); there will be a coherence between the literature review and the rest of thesis (again assuming the rest of the thesis is driven by the question(s)). The disadvantages are that there are no questions to drive the literature review itself; it could be the case that, unless the issues or problems that have initiated the research are so clearly defined as to determine the literature review, the review itself could be aimless and very hard to contain; there will a considerable delay before the empirical part of the research can be begun, because the literature review will have to be more or less completed first.

My suggestion is that you spend time on the generation of the research question(s) at the start of the research process. Even if you have only a reasonably clear question, you will be able to search in your literature review with purpose and direction. If it turns out that, as you explore the literature, you feel you need to change the research question(s), do so. In writing up, you can state the research question at the start of the thesis – conventionally in the introductory chapter – and again at the end of the literature review, to show that the question(s) does, indeed, emerge from the existing literature. You then have the advantage of preserving the coherence and structure of your thesis, and at the same time you are fairly clear, from the start of the research, where you are going.

A question emerging from an area of interest

One of my Masters students was searching for a focused topic for her dissertation. On Masters courses, there is usually little time for the development and exploration of research questions. Once the taught elements of the programme are completed, or perhaps even running alongside the beginnings of the dissertation work, the pressure of developing a research question and design are often very pressing for the one-year, or two-year part-time Masters student. This particular student wanted to research real-life contexts for second language learning, but was unsure how to frame a research question to begin the research. She began with three possible clusters of questions she wanted to address, all more-or-less related to each other:

1. Why does the real-life context yield worthwhile results for second language learners? What is the relationship between language learning and culture? How do sociologists define the concept of culture?
2. In real-life contexts, what aspects of culture affect your second language learning? How do you learn a second language (communicate with native speakers, watch TV programmes, do part-time jobs, residence with private families, join in social activities, etc.)?
3. Comparison of second language learning between the native real-life context and non-native speaking environments. Which is the most worthwhile: learning English as a second language in a native context or in a non-native speaking environment?

Let's work through these initial questions towards a manageable research question. First, I would suggest that we identify the most important question embedded here – or the one closest to the heart of the research interest. In the case of my student, it turned out to be in the third of her draft questions:

Which is the most worthwhile: learning English as a second language in a native context or in a non-native speaking environment?

The question suggests a comparative study: ideally, between second language learners in a native context and in a non-native speaking environment. But note that an emphasis on such a comparison sidelines the question of culture, which was where the student started her explorations in mapping the field of the research. For the purposes of the research, issues of culture – probably far too complex to handle within a six-month dissertation study – are put aside and embodied within a more manageable question: that of native vs non-native contexts for learning.

There is still a fairly complex concept within the emerging research question: the notion of 'worth'. To simplify, it would be possible to reframe the question: 'Which is better: learning English in a native context or in a non-native speaking environment?'. But the question still asks for a too-simple answer: is a native context better? Or is a non-native context better? (We would probably hypothesize that a native context was better.) The answer may be simple, but it may well also be simplistic. Instead, a better approach is to re-frame the question yet again to be *more sensitive to what is likely to be found* in empirical data-gathering. For example, 'What are the characteristics of learning a second language in a native context as opposed to a non-native context?'. Such a question suggests a clear, comparative research design, leading toward a list of characteristics of each approach as the kind of results we will be looking for. There is, however, one more problem with the question as it stands: are we sure that we can distinguish clearly between 'native' and 'non-native' contexts?

Native language-learning contexts are those, it is assumed, that occur naturally among speakers of, say, English as a first language. They could range from naturally occurring contexts like workplaces, homes, cafés and restaurants, bus stations and railway stations in the country in which English is the first language. Non-native contexts, on the other hand, are the opposite of these: where, for example, English is not the *lingua franca* nor the first language of discourse between people; where people are brought together to speak English for political or communication purposes (as when Indian people who speak different Indian languages meet and converse, or when Europeans from different language backgrounds converse at a conference in English). But are 'native' and 'non-native contexts' analogous to teaching situations with native speakers and non-native speakers? The assumption may be that they *are*, but the reality might well be that they *are not*. Further clarification will be required therefore, in the course of the thesis, about what exactly is meant by 'native' and 'non-native' in the research question.

3

Formulating Research Questions

Research questions can derive from the aims of a thesis. Here is a clear example of such derivation, from an investigation of children's writing in a Hong Kong primary school:

> The specific aims of this thesis are:
>
> First, to develop a broad theoretical framework within which HK children's writing can be analysed and described;
> Second, to develop a method of analysis to analyse HK children's (and perhaps other children's) writing systematically;
> Third, to use this method to explore and to describe what HK children do in their writing with particular reference to certain syntactic and textual aspects;
> Finally, to discuss the contribution and possible implications the study may have for the teaching of writing in English in HK.

How do these aims – which are well framed and lucid – translate into research questions? The temptation is to simply translate the wording into questions: 'What is a theoretical framework within which HK children's writing [in English] can be analysed and described?'. Indeed, that makes a very good research question, as would each of the aims translated simply into questions. The first lesson to be learnt from such translation is that *the aims of a thesis can be mirrored by the research questions*.

However, such translations do not always work as neatly as they might have done in the example discussed above. A factor to bear in mind with such translation is whether the research questions which derive from the aims are manageable and workable research questions. By 'manageable', I mean do they suggest a research methodology and is it likely that they can be answered in the course of the research project? By 'workable' is meant, are they of sufficient scale to be appropriate for the project in hand? Further questions that have to be asked are how do the questions relate to each other? Are there main and subsidiary questions in the set of questions?

Interestingly, the candidate who framed the aims described above did not undertake a straight translation from aims to research questions. Instead, these were what emerged:

> Put in another way, the thesis seeks to provide answer to the following research questions:
>
> 1. What do HK children do in their writing with regard to syntactic and textual aspects?
> 2. What would a method of analysis look like that enabled the syntactic and textual aspects of children's writing to be analysed systematically? What are its descriptive categories?
> 3. To a lesser extent: is there any discernible change over the age range in HK children's writing?
> 4. To a lesser extent: is there any discernible difference across genres in HK children's writing?

The first point to make about these research questions is that they are not the aims 'put in another way'. There is no reference to the aim 'to develop a broad theoretical framework within which HK children's writing can be analysed and described'. The first question – 'What do HK children do in their writing . . .?' invites a descriptive approach, which could be undertaken without recourse to theoretical reference. The second point is that the subsidiary questions, indicated by the phrase 'to a lesser extent', import new issues for consideration: one on the question as to whether there is change in the age range in HK children's writing, and one on differences across genres in the writing.

It cannot be said, therefore, that the aims are reflected clearly in the research questions, and vice versa. This may not be a problem in the course of the thesis, if either the aims or the research questions are used to inform the research; it will simply be the case that one or the other set will become redundant. But it could be the case that the research falls between two stools because neither the aims nor the research questions provide a clear starting point and foundation for the research. In fact, what happened in the thesis is that the subsidiary questions were not fully addressed and it might have been better to leave them out altogether. Furthermore, the first aim was not fully addressed, other than in an adequate literature review (but a 'broad theoretical framework' – why use *broad?* – was not *developed*).

The main aim would have been better cast as:

To explore and to describe what HK children do in their writing with particular reference to certain syntactic and textual aspects.

The research questions would follow from this over-arching aim:

Main question:

What do HK children do in their writing in English with regard to syntactic and textual aspects?

Subsidiary questions:

What would a theoretical framework look like within which HK children's writing in English might be analysed and described?
What would a method of analysis look like that enabled the syntactic and textual aspects of HK children's writing in English to be analysed systematically?

25

It can be seen from the above example that the subsidiary questions derive from the main question, and that the answers to them *contribute* to the answer to the main question. The relationship between the main and subsidiary question is clear.

Another example shows how a research question, with subsidiary questions, is formulated against the background of a problem that is identified as worth researching. In a doctoral thesis on multimedia approaches to teaching literature, the 'problem' was well set out. It consisted of the candidate's perception of the lack of guidance for multimedia teaching of literature, and his own sense of the need for further research in the field. The problem was multi-faceted, and was presented in the form of statements rather than questions. The main research question emerges from the context thus:

> The main area of research in the present thesis is whether multimedia technology can successfully explain the literary symbols that a human teacher, even with the help of other media, fails to explain and whether multimedia technology can help distance learners on their own.

This 'question' is not, in fact, a question – it is more of a statement. It contains two implied questions:

> Can multimedia technology successfully explain the literary symbols that a human teacher . . . fails to explain?

> Can multimedia technology help distance learners on their own?

These two questions overlap somewhat, though each would require a different methodology to answer them (the first suggests an experimental design in order to compare 'success'; the second requires an exploration of distance learners' practices and views). Because they are 'can' questions, the answer is probably 'yes' (with qualifications). It might have been better to couch these questions in slightly different terms:

26

To what extent does multimedia technology successfully explain . . .?
To what extent does multimedia technology help distance learners . . .?

Here, the assumption is that the technology does help in some way and the aim of the research is to find out what the nature of that help is.

The candidate's questions were followed by a sensitive discussion of the role of subsidiary questions in the research:

> Most substantial research has a main research question and a number of subsidiary questions to answer which crop up *passim* [in passing; in the course of the research] . . . Corollary issues that arise are: do teachers have non-textual resources available to explain the non-native symbols and do they use them? Do Indian students have the necessary training in 'reading' to elicit information from these media?

It is true that these are 'corollary issues that arise', but the danger is that such issues might simply be raised and then not explored by the research. If the raising of issues is an important and central part of the research, they are probably best discussed in the conclusion under 'Implications for practice/theory/policy/further research', rather than as pseudo research questions.

In yet another example of a research question emerging from a 'problem', the main research question is clearly stated – but with a secondary question attached:

> This thesis attempts to approach the problem of the learning and teaching of argument *via* narrative, asking the principal research question, 'What are the connections between the structures and composing processes associated with narrative and argumentative writing in the work of Year 8 students?' and secondly, 'Might narrative act as a bridge to argumentative writing?'. Various subsidiary questions emerge during the course of the research which will be discussed *passim.*

27

The main, or principal, research question is clearly and precisely stated, as well as being eminently researchable. But the secondary question is more of a metaphorical wish than a question, and might have been better cast as one of the aims of the research. It is interesting to note in this example that the subsidiary questions are not even set out at the start of the thesis: they are so subsidiary as to be a distraction at this point.

In the following example, from a Masters dissertation completed as part of a taught Masters course (i.e. a dissertation of 15–20 000 words), the research questions emerge clearly at the beginning of the dissertation:

> This dissertation will examine how the experience of returning to study affects mature women students. It poses, and attempts to give a reply to, three questions. The first is, why mature women feel the need to enter education again in the first place; the second is, how it affects their lives when they have done so and the third question asks how best they can be helped through the process.

The study does not operate with main and subsidiary questions: each question is as important as the other. The strength of this particular formulation is that the questions are clearly related to each other. Perhaps their strength derives in some part from the fact that the implicit main question for the dissertation is 'How does the experience of returning to study affect mature women students?'. Such a 'how' question invites the researcher to lay out the stages in answering the main question: why, how and how best? Of these three, the middle question is the central and main one. The first is contributory and the third looks at the implication for practice of the answer to the main question.

My final example in this section is taken from a doctoral study, the aim of which is 'to investigate the impact of the textual environment on two children, their conceptions of reading and what counts as texts in their daily experiences'. This is a particularly interesting example of how to formulate a research question, in that the question derives from a long and careful process of consideration of a field. The field – post-typographic (i.e. on-screen) reading behaviour – is a relatively recent one for researchers, and therefore is one in which the researcher has to map out the field and discuss how best to research it. There is little previous practice she can draw on. She begins with a rationale, then sets out 'four operational propositions' as the theoretical basis. These four claims act as the framework within which the actual research study can be formulated. Questions are asked along the way, e.g. 'concerning how the perspectives of preschool children, or children in their first years of school who proficiently use the Internet might differ from perspectives on text and reading of children who engage principally with print-based materials'. Such questions are used to create rhetorical and research space for the study, rather than as actual questions to be answered in the study.

The opening chapter moves gradually toward the asking of the main research question for thesis:

> How do the reading processes of two young readers differ across conventionally produced texts and multimedia, interactive digital texts?

The researcher goes on to state what the theoretical underpinning of the approach is, thus providing for the reader a clear account of the background against which the questions will be answered:

> Responding to the question requires a focus on two interrelated theoretical fields, reported in Chapters 2 and 3 respectively:
> * the typological and structural differences between print and interactive multimedia digital texts, and
> * the reading theories which have application to linear print only, and emergent theory which accommodates

nonlinear integrated compositions of media and interactive processing behaviours.

A major point emerging from this example is that a
research question plus an attendant methodology is not
enough to complete the main structure for a research
project; the other element required is reference to theory, or to a body of theoretical perspectives. Such mapping of the background to the study is important because
otherwise the research would proceed without *point* and
be open to the criticism 'Why are asking this question,
and why are you approaching it with this particular
methodology?'. To use the terminology and concepts of
the seminal thinker on argumentation, Toulmin (1958),
it is not enough to collect 'grounds' [evidence] to support your 'claims' [propositions, hypotheses, research
questions]. You need also to provide the 'warrant'
[means by which you link the evidence to the prop-
osition] and 'backing' [validation of the epistemological
– disciplinary and contextual - approach] in order to
build a strong argument in your thesis.

Other research questions

Examples of other research questions follow. They each
serve to demonstrate different aspects of the process of
formulating such questions in the design of research
projects. These examples come from work at Masters
level.

The first derive from a study of a Canadian–European
community programme for co-operation in higher education and training, and specifically from a collaboration
between The University of Prince Edward Island and The
University of York:

What are the different perceptions of the principal stakeholders involved in the programme?

> To what extent does an exchange programme have the potential to contribute to the professional development of citizenship education teachers?

These are two very different questions. The first one is typical of a Masters thesis in that it focuses on perceptions or attitudes. Such a focus enables a direct link with the methodology: if perceptions are what the researcher seeks, then she can ask via interview or questionnaire. All that needs to be defined is who the principal stakeholders are in this case. The second question is likely to be more problematic, in that measuring potential is a very inexact science: potential can be speculative, open-ended, even vague in its nature. Stakeholders may have differing views on potential and, if the potential is merely gauged on the basis of their perceptions, it would be relatively simple to record; but if the overall potential of a programme is to be measured, the researcher is up against the fact that potential is a future, idealistic phenomemon and, as such, cannot be measured. It might have been better to ask:

> To what extent does this particular exchange programme contribute to the professional development . . .?

or

> To what extent do participants in the programme perceive its potential to be?

in which case, the question is clearly subsidiary to the first, main question.

Another student poses her main question thus:

> What factors influence Chinese high school students to develop their English conversational skills?

This, in itself, is a very good question at Masters level. There is no attempt to determine which of the factors might be the most important, nor to prioritize the factors (though that would also be relatively manageable within a Masters thesis). However, the student then proceeds to add a number of further questions:

What are 'conversational skills'? What do Chinese students think are the elements of good English conversational skills?

What is the status of English conversational skills in current English teaching and learning in high schools in China?

What factors influence high school students to develop their conversational skills inside the classroom?

What factors influence high school students to develop their conversational skills outside the classroom?

The first of these further questions is definitional and might be left to discussion in the introduction of the thesis, or at some appropriate point. The second one – 'What do Chinese students think are the elements of good English conversational skills?' – is seemingly irrelevant to the main question, unless what the students *think* are the elements of the skills is actually a factor influencing the development of the skills. The third question, on the status of conversational skills in current teaching and learning, is also probably irrelevant. And the last two are clearly subsidiary, focussing as they do on factors inside and outside the classroom respectively.

4

Distinguishing Main from Subsidiary Questions

In this section I look at some examples of how research questions often appear in clusters in theses. In many theses, researchers work with a number of research questions, never entirely making clear whether one of the questions is more important than the others, or how the questions are related. Such a multiplicity of questions can lead to problems in the research and in the thesis.

Example 1

The Assessment of Comprehension Skills and Development of a Programme for Enhancing Comprehension Skills for Fourth Grade Students

The research questions in this thesis were defined early on, as part of the introduction. They followed closely the aims of the thesis and throughout there was general consistency in the use and application of the questions. The questions, as set out at the end of the introduction, were:

1. What are the comprehension learning needs of fourth grade pupils in [a particular country] and how can they be addressed?

2. What assessment techniques may be helpful in understanding reading comprehension?
3. Does the Reading and Thinking Strategies programme
adopted in this study affect pupils' performance on
reading comprehension?

The student goes on to say that the first question is to be
addressed in an exploratory phase of the empirical study;
the second question as part of the methodology and pilot
study; and the third by the main empirical study (the
results chapter). Each of these questions is answerable in
itself and, as such, each is a good research question. But
there are a number of problems, even at this early stage
in the thesis, and they are compounded as the thesis
develops and the student tries to answer the questions.

First, question 1 contains two questions: one on the
comprehension learning needs of fourth grade pupils
and a separate one on how these needs, once identified,
can be addressed. Each of these questions requires a
different approach in order to answer it. The first one is a
substantial needs analysis question. To answer it requires
a considerable amount of work and empirical research, as
each of the main elements of the question – needs,
comprehension, learning – are themselves complex enti-
ties. The second of these questions is a pedagogic and/or
strategic one: how can identified needs be addressed?
Because the question contains the word 'can', the answer
will be hypothetical. Needs can be addressed in a number
of ways, and the questions simply asks 'how can they be
addressed' in this particular context. It does not require
research to answer such a question, and is further evidence that 'can' questions might be best avoided in
research.

Second, there is a problem in that question 1 seems to
be the main question driving the thesis, with questions 2
and 3 being subsidiary or contributory to it. But any

hierarchical relationship between the three questions is not discussed. This is a problem common to many theses and dissertations. As the questions stand, the only assumption we can make as readers is that the three questions are equal in status. We don't know the situation, however, and more critically, neither does the student. She proceeds to move through the research and embark on the writing of the thesis without a clear sense of exactly where the thesis is going. Such multiple focus is confusing.

The student goes on to say that each of the three questions will be addressed in a different part of the thesis: the first in an exploratory study, the second as part of the methodology and the third in the main reporting of empirical results. There are methodological problems here. To attempt to answer one of the main research questions in a thesis with a preliminary and exploratory study is dangerous. In this case, the question was approached via 24 formal interviews. Although the interview schedule was tested with a panel of experts, the instrument was neither trialled nor piloted. There is therefore the likelihood that it could have been improved as a research tool. Furthermore, although the reliability of the instrument was fairly assured, the validity can be questioned because responses are short and do not explore the nature of the needs expressed.

It is particularly interesting that the student chooses to make her second research question, 'What assessment techniques may be helpful in understanding reading comprehension?', a methodological one – and suggests she will answer it in the chapter on the pilot study and methodology. This approach is unusual and risky in that it tries to do two things at once: test the research instrument for the main study *and* answer a research question about the most suitable assessment techniques in understanding reading comprehension. In fact, the two aims are not entirely compatible. The problem here is that neither aim is likely to be fulfilled satisfactorily. As has been stated earlier in this book, the main aim of a methodology and pilot study chapter is procedural; that is, its aim is to test the research instrument chosen to answer the main research question to see if it does the job well. It rarely can be trusted to give results of any worth; if it does, these have to be taken as provisional.

The third research question is a fine question in itself, and is answered in the thesis by an experimental design which sets up a control group and an experimental group to gauge the degree of effect of a metacognitive reading scheme on the comprehension abilities of young learners. The point to be made here is that any *one* of these three research questions could have provided the basis for an entire thesis or dissertation. It is confusing to list three without being explicit about the relations between them, whether those relations are sequential and/or hierarchical.

Example 2

Writing Demands across the Transition from Primary to Secondary School

In this particular thesis, mentioned earlier, the research questions emerge at the end of the literature review and are not stated until that point in the thesis. The study looks at issues of transition, continuity and progression in the English National Curriculum and, as such, initially identifies a problem, *viz* that continuity is, at best, patchy, and, at worst, poor between primary and secondary schooling in England. There follows a literature review chapter on the conceptualization of progression in writing, the particular focus of the study. When the research questions emerge, they are clearly generated by the literature review:

1. Is there a difference in the ways writing is taught and used in primary and secondary schools, as pupils move from Year 6 to Year 7? The subsidiary question is whether preparation for the Key Stage 2 tests [the National Curriculum in England and Wales is divided into four key stages. Key Stage 2 includes 7–11-year-old children] affects the teaching of writing in Year 6.
2. What are the similarities or differences in the writing processes that pupils experience in Years 6 and 7?
3. What are the differences and similarities in pupils' perceptions of writing in Years 6 and 7?
4. What do the answers to these questions tell us about transition and progression as pupils move from primary to secondary school?

The chapter ends with a signposting statement: 'The next chapter will describe the methodology used to investigate these questions'.

There is no doubting the clarity or provenance of these questions. They emerge from the student's experience as a teacher and also from the review of the literature; they are a distillation from these two sources. Questions 1–3 define different areas of enquiry. The first is on 'the ways writing is taught', the second on 'similarities or differences in ... writing processes' and the third on 'differences and similarities in pupils' perceptions of writing'. The fourth question is a more general one: 'What do [these answers] tell us about transition and progression as pupils move from primary to secondary school?'. The relationship between the four questions is fairly clear: questions 1–3 lead to question 4. Put another way, question four is the main research question, and might have been re-cast as 'What do we know about transition and progression *in writing* as pupils move from primary to secondary school *in England*?'. Such a re-casting makes it clear to us that questions 1–3 are subsidiary to this main question, each investigating a particular aspect of it. Subsidiary questions of this kind are also contributory in that they contribute to the answering of the main question. This particular set of research questions is complicated, however, by the addition of a subsidiary question as part of question 1: the subsidiary question is whether preparation for the Key Stage 2 tests affects the teaching of writing in Year 6. Here I think we have an example of how a seemingly minor subsidiary research question could have thrown the whole thesis off balance. It is a big question, because gauging the effect of Key Stage 2 tests on writing in Year 6 would need a substantial experimental study. As it turns out, the student does not fully address this subsidiary question so perhaps it would have been better not to raise the question at all.

The thesis concludes with a return to the first three questions, treating each of them in some depth. Such unity of structure and purpose says much about the general coherence of the thesis as a whole.

How to avoid problems in designing your research questions

It is almost inevitable that a number of questions will come to mind when embarking on a research project. These might emerge from brainstorming, from a review of the literature, in the course of the research, or in other ways. Is it worth giving vent to these various questions, as they are all probably related in some way to your emerging research. A key question to consider, however, is how are they related? And is one the questions the main question that is firing your curiosity and which, in due course, will determine the methodology, structure and nature of your study?

Once the questions present themselves, a good way to assess them is to write them out on separate strips of paper (or list them in a single computer file). Experiment with moving the questions so that they seem to make sense in relation to each other. Does one of them seem like the main question? Are some more general or more specific than others? How do they stand in relation to each other? Can some of them be omitted, or fused, or added to?

Ideally, if you still have a number of questions you want to research, you should work towards a main question and subsidiary questions. For example, in the following set of questions, which one seems to be the main one? All refer to the teaching of English as a second language in a primary school:

What are the perceptions, the processes and the experiences of the teaching of English as a second language in a primary school?

What are the teaching methods that teachers use in the classroom for the acquisition of English?

Why do teachers use these teaching methods for the acquisition of English?

What are the teaching methods that pupils prefer the teachers to use for the acquisition of English?

Why do pupils prefer the teachers to use some teaching methods over others?

What other school processes may contribute to the acquisition of English?

What do teachers and pupils believe about the contribution of these school processes to the acquisition of English?

It is sometimes difficult for a student to work out which is his or her main question, and which are subsidiary. From a list of seven questions, like those above, it is essential to look for some more general patterns in the generation of the questions, so as to put them in relation to each other. For example, the relationship could be determined, as shown in Figure 4.1.

The first point to make about this emerging pattern and design is that the main research question, with its emphasis on perceptions, processes and experiences, is not reflected in the subsidiary questions, which focus on methods and processes. In this example, then, it might be

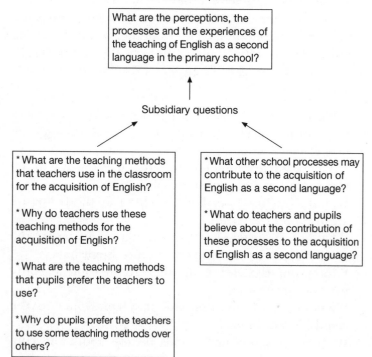

Figure 4.1 Main and subsidiary questions 1.

better to change the main research question to 'What are the methods and processes . . .?'.

An interesting point – and a potential difficulty – is that each cluster of the subsidiary questions could act as the basis for a research study in its own right. Indeed, there are two such clusters in the 'methods' box: one on teachers' perspectives and another on pupils' perspectives. In designing the relationship and status of questions asked, it will have to be borne in mind that these more specific questions on methods and processes are secondary to the main research question and should not take over as the main questions for the research project. This point leads on to a third one.

The questions asked in the subsidiary boxes could almost constitute the beginnings of interview or questionnaire questions. In fact, some of them could translate directly on to an interview or questionnaire protocol. In generating such questions at the start of a project, the researcher needs to ask him- or herself whether he or she is actually forming questions that will be asked of respondents, rather than shaping research questions for the study as a whole.

In general, it is best not to have too many main and subsidiary questions in the design of a research project, because each of these questions will have to be answered in the course of the research – and answered well. Furthermore, supervisors and examiners will be interested in how the various questions relate to each other.

A better, refined version of the design for the example discussed above might be as shown in Figure 4.2.

Throughout the distinction between 'methods' and 'processes' will have to be made; otherwise it might be better to simplify the design by just concentrating on 'methods', which will be more easily observable or researchable. If the researcher wanted to delimit the scope of the study even more, he or she could concen-

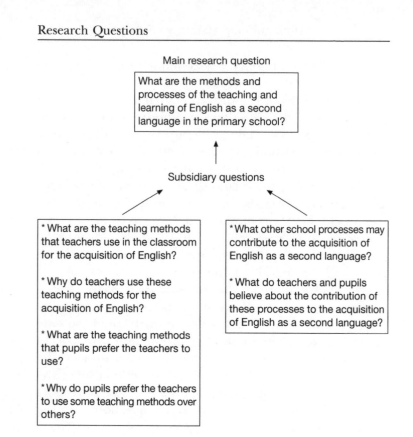

Main research question

What are the methods and processes of the teaching and learning of English as a second language in the primary school?

Subsidiary questions

* What are the teaching methods that teachers use in the classroom for the acquisition of English?

* Why do teachers use these teaching methods for the acquisition of English?

* What are the teaching methods that pupils prefer the teachers to use?

* Why do pupils prefer the teachers to use some teaching methods over others?

* What other school processes may contribute to the acquisition of English as a second language?

* What do teachers and pupils believe about the contribution of these processes to the acquisition of English as a second language?

Figure 4.2   Main and subsidiary questions 2.

trate on teaching, and therefore on teachers' responses, rather than try to look at both teaching and learning. Again, if both are to be looked at, there will need to be consideration of their relationship: in the definitions of terms, the literature review and in the analysis of data generated from the empirical study.

Integrating answers to main and subsidiary questions

It is one thing to ask questions clearly; it is another to deal with the answer to these questions. If research questions are clearly formulated and consideration is given to the relationship between them at the outset of the research, it makes life a great deal more easy when it comes to analysing the answer to the questions. There are two places in a dissertation or thesis where such integration and discussion can take place: in the 'Discussion' section (which sometimes appears as a separate section and sometimes as part of the 'Results' chapter(s)), or in the 'Conclusion'.

If subsidiary questions are essential in answering aspects of the research *on the way to* answering the main research questions, then they should be addressed first. An appropriate approach would be to go through the subsidiary questions, setting out what the answers are and discussing their implications as part of the bigger picture. There might be a logical sequence suggested in both the posing and the answering of questions. For example, in the case of the project on second language learning in the primary school, it is clear that discussion of the teaching methods used in the classroom should preface the discussion of why teachers use these methods.

If, on the other hand, the subsidiary questions follow from the main question – and are, in effect, ancillary questions as opposed to contributory ones – then their discussion is best after that of the main question. It is important to remember that such questions are an integral part of the research design, and thus must be addressed before a consideration of implications for further research, policy and/or practice, which may arise in the form of further questions generated by the research.

In some cases, during the course of a research project, it turns out that a subsidiary question generates more interesting and important data than the original main question. It should still be reported as a subsidiary, though implications for further research (perhaps in another research study) will be considerable. Such changes of emphasis within the course of a research project are common, but once the research design is established, after careful work at the literature review stage and pilot stages of the empirical study, the researcher should stick to the original design. It is not sensible to discuss a subsidiary question as if it is the main question, and as a consequence, to let the main question fade into insignificance.

5

Contributory Questions

I made the distinction in the last section between, on the one hand, *subsidiary* questions that derive from a main question and which should be answered (in the writing up) after the answering of the main question; and, on the other hand, *contributory* questions that work toward the answering of the main question – and therefore should be answered before the answering of the main question. In the present section, I want to focus on these contributory questions, and will use an example of their use to discuss the key issues.

In forming research questions in difficult, new or under-explored areas, it is often hard to get a purchase on exactly how to approach the problem. The definition of a main research question may take some time, especially if there is not much of a research literature to draw on. There may be a need for exploratory empirical work and, indeed, for a different paradigmatic approach to the whole research project. Whereas conventionally, research tends to be conceived empirically as a pyramid, with (for example) a large sample being surveyed first, a sub-sample being interviewed later, and perhaps a sub-sub-sample being examined in a case study later, as in Figure 5.1, in exploratory research an inverted pyramid suggests a more appropriate approach (Figure 5.2).

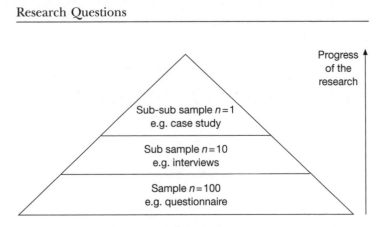

Figure 5.1 The 'pyramid' approach to empirical research.

Typically, in the conventional approach, a question-naire survey might be carried out as a first stage of a main study in order to answer a broad set of questions. The sample might be, say, 100. Following the administering of the instrument and an analysis of the questionnaire results, a sub-sample of ten might be selected for in-depth, semi-structured interviews. Again, results would be transcribed and analysed. Finally, as a third stage, a single case study might be undertaken to explore in more depth some of the issues that had arisen. Different research designs can be worked out from such a model: for example, a study could be based only on ten interviews and a case study; or only on one of these levels. It is unlikely, however, that a large-scale questionnaire and one or two case studies would be combined in a research design, as such a configuration would be open to criti-cisms of selection bias in the move from the large-scale to the very small-scale levels. A consistent factor to bear in mind, and which is reinforced by the pyramid metaphor, is proportionality.

Imagine an *inverted* pyramid (Figure 5.2). In this case, the research starts with something as informal as a con-versation with a single person or a fully-fledged study of a

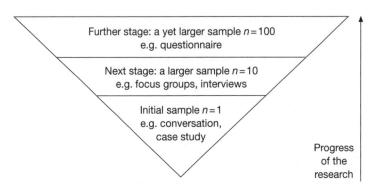

Further stage: a yet larger sample *n* = 100
e.g. questionnaire

Next stage: a larger sample *n* = 10
e.g. focus groups, interviews

Initial sample *n* = 1
e.g. conversation,
case study

Progress
of the
research

Figure 5.2 The 'inverted pyramid' approach to empirical research.

single case. As issues and questions are explored and
refined, the research moves on to test its hunches and
suppositions with a larger sample – say with a group of
ten interviewees or with a focus group or two. Its main
aim is clarification of these issues and questions, and
initial exploration of the various factors or variables that
are at play. Once these issues and questions have been
clarified, it may be appropriate to test them with a larger
sample – say 100 – in questionnaire form. The project
could even be extended to 1000 respondents.

In the inverted pyramid design, the relationship of
contributory questions to a main question is obvious: by
asking a number of initial questions, a sharper sense of
the whole direction of the research can be honed, with a
single, main research question or hypothesis emerging in
due course. But contributory questions can be used with
either model.

One current PhD thesis on which I am an adviser has
gradually worked towards a model in which contributory
questions come first and lead toward the answering of a
main question. The progress towards a main question
has not been easy, because the field is notoriously hard to
research at present: it is the field of web-based self-access

additional language learning. The main research question has been formulated as:

> What are the pedagogical challenges that teachers have been facing with the introduction of web-based self-access material in the teaching and learning of foreign languages in a higher education language centre?

First, it has to be said that this is an excellent research question. It is a 'what' question: the answer(s) will take the form of a set of challenges that teachers have been facing. These are likely to be complex, so it will not a simple matter of a neat list. The answers are likely to be multi-factored, contingent on context and circumstance and dependant on a number of underpinning definitions. But at least we know, at this stage, that the researcher is clear about the parameters of the study.

In order to answer the question, however, the researcher has worked out that a number of contributory questions have to be answered first. These are couched in the draft introduction as 'subsidiary' questions, which they indeed are; but they are a particular kind of subsidiary question: ones that will help to answer the main one. They are:

> What are the pedagogical issues behind the design, organisation and compilation of web-based self-access language learning material?

> What is the role of the teachers, learners and computers when using web-based self-access language learning material in the teaching and learning of foreign languages?

and

> What are the pedagogical and practical changes that foreign language tutors need to undertake in order to enhance the use of web-based self-access language learning material to support the learning of the target language?

When the subsidiary questions derive from the main

question, the overall research design follows from the main research question; in this case the research methods chosen are appropriate to the individual contributory questions. The researcher is careful to point out in the course of her thesis which parts of her methodology answer which contributory questions. In relation to the above three contributory questions, the following methods were used: semi-structured questionnaires, semi-structured interviews and e-lab session observations respectively. Once these are answered satisfactorily, she can move toward the answering of the main questions. Rather like Polonius' advice to Ophelia in *Hamlet*, a supervisor's advice in this case might be to say: 'by indirections find directions out'.

The key in such an approach is to make sure that, once the contributory questions are answered, these answers are brought together to address the main question. Do they, in fact, help to answer that question? Or do they fall short of an overall answer, individually and/or collectively? Do further contributory answers need to be asked before an answer to the main question can be found? In the end, does the main research question remain the most important question, or is one or more of the contributory questions more revealing and interesting than had originally been thought? These last few questions are best discussed in a Discussion section at the end of the presentation of results, or in a Conclusion.

Sometimes, in the presentation and writing up of research results, researchers and students forget to bring together the various component parts of their study. They assume that the parts make up the whole, and almost leave it up to the reader to make the required connections or ask the pertinent questions. It is much better to make those connections explicit within a conventional research paradigm (or to leave them unconnected in an unconventional one). If in doubt, follow W. B. Yeats' advice: 'ancient salt is best packing'. In other words, use conventional and well-tried structuring and packaging if you want to say something new (as most research does).

Such bringing together of the answers gained from different methods and from different questions is a form of triangulation. As the researcher says in her draft:

> The use of multiple methods to conduct the present research study [addressed] the subsidiary questions, and [allowed me] to triangulate the data gathered through the interviews, questionnaires and observations.

There is a clear relationship between the subsidiary (contributory) questions and the main one in this study. Such clarity may not emerge early in the course of the research – in this case, not until the transfer from MPhil to PhD about two-thirds of the way through the project as a whole – but it must emerge before the final thesis is presented for examination.

If such clarity does not emerge, it is perfectly possible to say that further research is needed to determine the relationship between variables or to refine the research questions yet further. Within the confines of a registration period for a higher degree, it may not be possible to answer main and/or subsidiary questions satisfactorily. Such incompletion is not necessarily the researcher's fault; it may lie in the inherent complexity and/or relatively unexplored nature of the field that is being researched.

6

How Research Questions Determine the Methodology of a Thesis

Sometimes research questions emerge gradually in the course of a research project and to force their emergence too soon can send a researcher in the wrong direction. In one particular case, a researcher had completed her Masters thesis successfully and wished to move on immediately to register for an MPhil/PhD. She felt that the most interesting topic was the impact of information and communication technologies on (young women's) second language learning of English in Taiwan, and embarked on a three-year full-time exploration of this topic. The present section is the story of how the project changed and how the research question(s) changed to reflect the overall realignment of priorities.

Changes as a result of reading

It was clear from the start that there were three main areas of interest, and that the relationship between these areas was to be the focus of the research. These three areas were a) English language learning, as a second/foreign language, b) the effect or impact of information and communication technologies on such learning and c) women's status and access to such learning in Taiwan.

51

The relationship between the three elements could be depicted as shown in Figure 6.1.

At this early stage in the research, the main axis of attention seemed to be along the top of the triangle. In other words, the focus was to be on how ICT could help language learning, with Taiwanese young women being the population for the research. The rationale for the focus of the research was as follows:

> My earlier study on pupils' views concerning learning English showed that using computers and the Internet, watching films on television and listening to popular English songs, were frequently mentioned as the means by which pupils had experience of using English and the reasons why they liked to learn English. The pragmatic use and ultimate goal of language – communication,

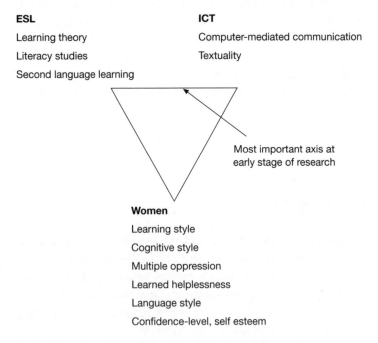

ESL
Learning theory
Literacy studies
Second language learning

ICT
Computer-mediated communication
Textuality

Most important axis at early stage of research

Women
Learning style
Cognitive style
Multiple oppression
Learned helplessness
Language style
Confidence-level, self esteem

Figure 6.1 Identifying the main axis for research.

whether to foreigners or classmates in daily conversation or letters – was also regarded as an interesting and motivating experience. These findings indicated that learning English through the combination of communication and technology (ICT) may be a possible way to increase pupils' motivation and help them learn effectively.

The research questions which emerged from this interest were based very much on the Masters level work:

Main question:

Do electronic media (films, electronic books, computer games and other electronic communication) have better effects in helping young learners learn English than conventional media (books, printed text)?

Subsidiary questions:

To explore the prevalence of using conventional media and electronic media to learn English among young learners.
To explore the attitudes of learners towards conventional and electronic media to learn English. Do electronic media have greater influence in motivating learners to learn English?
To explore the learning strategies employed when using conventional and electronic media to learn English.
To explore the types of language knowledge acquired through conventional and electronic media
To explore the types of culture knowledge acquired through conventional and electronic media.
To explore the methods and possibility of combining conventional and electronic media to teach English to young learners.

While most of the subsidiary questions are not, in fact, questions – they are more like objectives – there is a question buried in them that looks more like a candidate for a main research question, in that it is well focused and researchable: 'Do electronic media have a greater influence [than conventional media] in motivating [Taiwanese] learners to learn English?'. This question, is, however, different from the proposed main question,

53

which is about the *effects* of electronic media. A question about effects, given the wide-ranging nature of the area (electronic vs conventional media in learning) is likely to be harder to answer, even within a three-year full-time (or five- to six-year part-time) doctoral project.

Another attempt to define the focus of the research took a slightly different line, and sheds further light on the formulation of research questions at early stages of a research project. The original conception of comparing learning via electronic media and learning via conventional media suggested that an 'effect' question might be a good one to pursue:

> Do literature reading and the Internet for Taiwanese EFL students have a positive effect on their English learning?

Again, the emphasis on effect was pushing the research down a particular line. This particular question was problematic in that regard because it was asking two effect questions: 'Does literature reading ... have a positive effect?' and 'Does the Internet ... have a positive effect?'. Although each of these causal questions would have been answerable, considerable refining of the definitions of 'literature reading' and 'the Internet' would have been necessary. A related question that would have required a different design for the research would be:

> What are the advantages and disadvantages of literature reading and the Internet for Taiwanese high school students' learning?

Thus moving the design of the study away from the scientific cause-and-effect paradigm to a (perhaps) more manageable design, leading, in the end, to answer the question via a conceptual grid (as shown in Figure 6.2).

At this stage of the emerging research project, an empirical study was being considered, with a questionnaire survey of 150–200 of junior (14–16) or senior high (17–19) school students followed by in-depth interviews

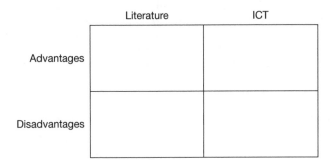

Figure 6.2   Conceptual grid.

with a 10 per cent sub-sample of 15–20 students in four or five schools in Taiwan. This would have made a researchable and feasible project in three years, with its emphasis on students' views, an appropriate pilot study, and a fairly conventional research methodology.

About six months into the MPhil/PhD research, however, the aspect of women's experience of language learning began to take on more prominence for the researcher, both personally and intellectually. Its emergence added a significant dimension to the research project as a whole. The clearly stated rationale above gave rise to the following topic, given the interest in women's language learning: 'How can ICT help women's language learning in Taiwan?' This, in turn, generated a research question: 'What impact do ICT, ideology and cultural hegemony have on women learning English in Taiwan?', thus framing the project within feminist literature. The subsidiary questions began to set out the interests of the research in more detail:

What is the role of English in the construction of gender and power in Taiwan?
What are women's views about and experiences of power within the [prevailing] ideology?
What are language learners' experience of and views

55

about ICT, hegemony and cultural industry and how do
they influence their acquisition of languages?
How can policy be made based on the ideology at work to
benefit women and their learning?
What are the implications of ideology, ICT and cultural
hegemony for women's English learning? Of what use
might these three be to women's English learning?

Such a set of questions suggested the need for three
literature reviews: one on Taiwan and hegemony; one on
gender and language learning; and one on ICT. They
appeared originally in that order, with a gradual sifting
and re-arranging taking place as the ideas generated by
the reading brought about a subtle re-orientation in the
approach. For example, material on Taiwan and on language learning were gradually moved from the second
chapter, where they seemed to grow from an increasing
interest (and wider reading) about gender and schooling,
to the first and third chapters respectively, so that second
language learning became linked more closely with ICT
(thus helping to delimit the literature search) and more
space was created for literature on gender issues.

At this point in the research, with a sometimes sudden
and sometimes gradual shift taking place towards a principal interest in gender issues, various other research
questions were drafted to try to define exactly the focus
and direction of the research. One of the particularly
interesting ones was:

Does English learning lead women to independence and
a better future without oppression or does it lead them to
serve the patriarchy and capitalist system with their English expertise and then lose themselves in the dominant
cultural monopoly by being materialised?

This question might be best defined, in hindsight, as not
so much an alternative research question, as indicative of
issues that were to become more central to the research:
what is nature of the patriarchical system in Taiwan and

how is it different from global capitalist hegemonies? Do Taiwanese women 'lose themselves', i.e. lose identity, as they are enculturated into English?

The centrality of gender issues to the research project is also indicated by the specific nature of the subsidiary questions, listed above. What was happening in the development of the research was that ICT, originally a key element in the central axis of thinking about the direction of the research, was gradually being sidelined in favour of a focus on gender and second language learning (with ICT as an aspect of language learning). Other aspects of gender – patriarchy and identity/women's self-esteem – came more to the fore. In the next sub-section, the impact of the early stages of the empirical data collection is gauged on the emerging research question(s).

Changes as a result of empirical research

When there are three main areas of interest, albeit fluctuating in their prominence and relationship, it is hard to know how best to design a methodology to answer the main research question – especially as the question itself is unstable. Consequently, a methodological approach was designed to help sharpen the focus of the research. To complicate matters further, the methodology itself changed.

The empirical work began about one year into the three-year project, after the first year was spent in thinking through the conceptual basis for the study and undertaking extensive reading and note-taking (and first-draft writing of the chapters of the literature review). To begin with, the empirical study was conceived in terms of a pre-pilot using a focus group, followed by a pilot using the

57

full range of intended methods for the main part of the study.

The advantage of using a focus group for the first stage of the empirical study is that it allows the exploration of ideas as well as the testing of a particular method. Another title in the series looks specifically at the methodology of the focus group in education and social science research (Litosseliti, 2003). As far as the present discussion is concerned, it was the data that emerged from the focus group in the form of a mutually enlightening conversation between five Taiwanese women studying at a British university that proved critical in the development of the research.

What emerged during the conversation, despite carefully prepared protocols or schedules of questions designed to concentrate attention on the original three main areas of interest in the research, was that issues of gender, patriarchy, identity and language-learning were paramount for the respondents and that use of ICT was relatively peripheral. Indeed, it appeared that radio and television were more commonly used than computer-based ICT to support language learning. It was as if, in the very process of initial data collection, a new focus for the research was being created.

Considerable thought must be given to moments like this, because the last thing a researcher or his or her supervisor(s) want is an ever-changing focus for the research. But on this occasion, the results of the focus group seemed to be bringing the researcher closer to his or her own desired intention: the exploration of gender, identity and language learning within a Taiwanese patriarchal context. At this point, the main axis of interest in the research had shifted from that of language and ICT to that of gender and language, with the third element – ICT – playing a secondary role.

Such a shift also had implications for the structure as well as the methodology of the thesis. Plans were for it now to begin with a personal statement, in the tradition of some kinds of qualitative research, where the researcher sets out his or her position so as to acknowledge the influence he or she has on the research. Then the literature review needed to be realigned, with chapters on the Taiwanese context, on gender/literacy and on ICT following the introduction. Finally, the emerging methodology needed to be clarified. Figure 6.3 illustrates the design of the empirical study. Whereas the original design for the empirical study had imagined that a pre-pilot and pilot study would prepare the ground, methodologically, for the main study (as is the classic function of pilot studies, i.e. a process function), it now turned out

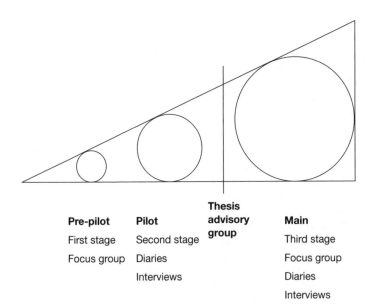

Pre-pilot	Pilot	Thesis advisory group	Main
First stage	Second stage		Third stage
Focus group	Diaries		Focus group
	Interviews		Diaries
			Interviews

Figure 6.3 Research design for an evolving study.

59

that the substantial data collected in the pre-pilot warranted its consideration in the final analysis of the data. So rather than conceive the design of the empirical study as consisting conventionally of a pilot study and main study, the newly fashioned design consists of three stages: the first being the 'pre-pilot', the second being the 'pilot' and the third the 'main study'. The pilot stages still serve the purpose of testing the research instruments, but they also provide valuable substantial data in the attempt to answer the main question. Progress towards an answer, then, will evolve. In the end, the thesis might help us to understand better the relationship between the three elements in the original conception: gender, second language learning and ICT. The research question has been refined to:

> What is the impact of gender and ICT on Taiwanese female students' English learning in a British University in Britain?

with gender as the dominant issues and ICT as a secondary one. Subsidiary questions become:

> What is the role of English in the construction of gender and power relations?
> What are women's views and experiences within the prevailing ideology?
> What are Taiwanese female students' experiences of and views about ICT, gender and hegemony, and how do these influence their acquisition of language learning?
> What possible changes in ideology might benefit women and their learning?
> What are the implications of gender ideology and ICT for women's language learning?

A process of gradual transformation has led to the above set of research questions. Some of the factors have been pragmatic (for example, the fact that it became clear that the empirical part of the study was best conducted in the

UK rather than in Taiwan, for personal and financial reasons); others have been conceptual (the shift towards an interest in feminist perspectives on second language acquisition). Each of the shifts discussed in this section have led to a different relationship between the research question(s) and the proposed structure and methodology of the research and its eventual thesis. Such a symbiotic relationship is common, as the aim is to achieve a thesis which is coherent, elegant, well-designed according to its purpose, rigorous and clearly addressing a research question. The final conception of the thesis discussed above led to a provisional structure for the chapters as shown in Figure 6.4.

This unusual structure (normally one might expect the literature review chapters to be more equal in length, the methodology and pilot study chapter to be shorter and the 'results' chapter(s) to be of roughly equivalent length) reflects the need for the thesis to follow the researcher's intentions and design. The research question is best answered by such a structure, which gives due

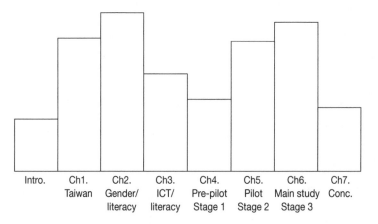

Figure 6.4 Structure of thesis.

weight to the centrality of gender in the research project and the developed methodology, which builds, stage by stage, to an ever more substantial and insightful answer to the main research question.

7

Problems with Research Questions

Problems can occur with the writing of a thesis or dissertation if research questions are not clear from near the start of the project. I can think of one thesis which I took over from another supervisor when it was about half-finished. It had progressed seemingly well, with about two-thirds of the first draft and all of the empirical work completed. Research questions did not seem to be an issue. The thesis was focused on language policy in Hong Kong. The student was conscientious, insightful and hard-working. It appeared that the rest of the supervision would simply be a matter of seeing the project through to its successful completion.

However, as the data was analysed and as presentations of the work in progress began to be made at postgraduate seminars, it became clear that the research questions needed to be re-visited. They originally took the form of a long list of questions:

1. What is the impact of the medium of instruction policy on academic results in general subjects?
2. What is the impact of the medium of instruction policy in language subjects (both Chinese and English)?
3. What are the cultural implications of the new medium of instruction policy for students?
4. What are the pedagogical implications of eliminating code-mixing and putting forward a pure language teaching medium?

5. What are the political implications of eliminating code-mixing and putting forward a pure language teaching medium?
6. Is a bilingual model feasible in Hong Kong? If this is practical, then what model should be adopted?

This is an interesting set of questions – all of them are important, and all answerable in their different ways. Part of the problem with this set is that to answer all the questions would take several research projects (or one much larger and more wide-ranging than an individual doctoral project). Let's unravel some of the implications of these questions.

The first two focus on the *impact* of the 1998 Hong Kong language policy. This policy proposed the creation of English Medium of Instruction schools and Chinese Medium of Instruction schools. Of these two, the first one requires the gathering and analysis of statistical data from examination results in order to gauge the impact that a change of policy has made. Such an analysis would be relatively straightforward: results from 1998 and after could be compared with 1997 and before. A reasonably long time-scale would have to be used, as results would not change overnight (for example, students starting secondary school in 1998 might not take their end-of-school examinations until 2003). Answering the research question is relatively straightforward in this case because the aim is to measure the impact of a single intervention on a single factor or variable: examination results. In the second question, however, the measurement of impact is more problematic if the focus is not on results, but on the general teaching and learning within language subjects, on numbers enrolled in different language subjects, and across language subjects. In other words, the second question is less well defined and raises difficult questions over the key word in the question as far as methodology is concerned: *impact*. For a discussion of this term, see earlier sections.

The third question, 'What are the cultural implications of the new medium of instruction policy for students?' is a good research question in itself, suitable in scale for a doctoral thesis. The difficult and interesting word in the question is 'cultural'. There would need to be considerable discussion in the early part of the thesis, referring to previous discussion of the term and its meanings and, most probably, delimiting the meanings for the purpose of the research. Because the question is looking at *implications* rather than *effects* or *impact*, there is freedom and scope for the researcher to explore the implications of an intervention (the new medium of instruction policy) without the constraint of having to determine and analyse an end result of any kind. Whereas *implications* are often addressed at the end of a thesis, as part of the conclusion to a piece of research, there is nothing to stop an entire research project being devoted to the implications of an intervention or possible intervention for a particular population. This question, then, is sufficient for a thesis in its own right.

The next two questions address a similar issue: the elimination of code-mixing (i.e. using Chinese and English interchangeably in conversation and other discourses) and the concentration on a 'pure' or single medium of instruction in schools. One question addresses the pedagogical implications of such a move, while the other addresses the political implications. It is good to separate these possible implications, even though they might be related. One has to assume that the elimination of code-mixing *is* directly related to the promotion of 'pure' medium of instruction schooling to make a worthwhile comparison and here the potential problem is that code-mixing may be a part of everyday conversational discourse and not strictly comparable with formal language use in schools. But if that problem can be resolved, the questions look answerable via questionnaire, interview and other investigative methods. Again, these two in themselves might be the basis on which an entire thesis is built.

Finally, the last question is actually two questions: first, is a bilingual model feasible in Hong Kong? Second, if this [i.e. a bilingual model] is practical, then what model [i.e. what version?] should be adopted? Questions like the first of these – is a bilingual model feasible? – can often be answered by 'yes' or 'no', or 'yes' with qualifications. As such, they do not provide very helpful *research* questions because they could be answered quickly on the basis of a set of evidence that is hastily marshalled. Note that the second question is slightly different and does not follow on from the first (as perhaps the candidate assumed it would). It asks, If this model is *practical*, what version of it should be adopted? Feasibility is not necessarily the same as practicality. Note also the slippage taking place in the use of the deictic *this* to refer back to what we have to assume is the bilingual model, and then the consequent and confusing question, What *model* should be adopted? Our own conclusion should be that neither of these questions is a good research question because both are unfocused and not very clearly related to each other.

The problems identified above can be summarized thus: there were eight questions in all, not clearly related to each other, some requiring one methodological approach and others another. Some questions were better than others as research questions; and two or three of the questions would have provided more than enough of a starting point for an entire doctoral thesis.

The problems were compounded by what followed in an early draft of the thesis. The questions appeared near the beginning of the thesis. They then re-appeared near the beginning of the chapter on methodology and the pilot study, but *in a different form,* this time reduced to four questions. They then appeared again at the beginning of the first of two chapters based on the results of data collection, once again in a slightly different form. Two of the four distilled questions were answered (one better than the other) and the other two were not mentioned again. The problem with such an approach to the use of research questions is that each time a question is asked, expectations are raised as to the answers to such questions. If these expectations are not met, disappointment and confusion ensues. To make matters even worse, in the particular case we are discussing, two further questions appeared in the introduction which seemed rhetorical in nature, i.e. never intending to be answered but simply asked for interest's sake in passing. It is worthwhile, whenever asking a question in the writing of a thesis to ask yourself: what is the status of this question? Am I asking it as a rhetorical move, or do I genuinely intend to answer it in the course of the research? If so, how am I going to answer it? Do I come back to it later in the thesis to check my progress in answering it – and, in the end, to trying to answer it?

In the case described above, the final version of the research questions was exemplary for its clarity and its strategic use within the thesis.

Questions that are not questions

Sometimes students set out a series of 'questions' for the conduct of their research that are not, in fact, questions at all. They are statements. The problem with statements (to be distinguished from hypotheses) is that they do not readily translate into mechanisms for driving the research design, the methodology or the overall structure of the research.

In the following example, the student seems to be at the stage of identifying issues and 'areas of concern' (or problems) in a particular field, even though these statements are called 'questions':

> Music in the National Curriculum [in England and Wales] is general, but some teachers implement the curriculum in a narrow or particular way.
> Within the whole school curriculum, music would appear to be given less emphasis than most other subject disciplines.

These statements give rise to two main areas of concern, which 'motivate this enquiry':

> reasons for divergent practice, and trying to understand the nature of the diversity and the underlying reasons for it. These may include the influence of existing resources, teachers' attitudes, accepted professional traditions or an explicit rationale for music education;
> a consideration of the place and status of music in schools; to find out to what extent a range of teachers within school communities share a similar perception of music education.

In this case, further development of the research idea would need to take place to determine what the keystone of the research is: whether, for instance, it is the question of reasons for divergent practice ('What are the reasons for divergent practice in music education in secondary schools in England and Wales?'); or whether it is a question of the place and status of music in schools; or, indeed, whether it is about common perceptions of music education. Each of these questions would require a different methodological approach and a different literature review.

Mistaking interview or questionnaire questions for research questions

It is useful to make a distinction between questions that are used in an interview protocol or a questionnaire on the one hand, and research questions on the other. A research question might not be actually asked in the course of a research project, though at some point it may well be advantageous to ask the overall research question directly to your respondents (many students seem to avoid asking the 'overwhelming question').

Some students, in beginning to generate research questions at the start of a project, seem to create potential interview or questionnaire questions instead. In other words, the questions are too specific. The following example, on the topic of students' perceptions of the role of examinations, falls into this category:

> Does having to take examinations make you work harder, make no difference or put you off?
> Do exams affect you differently if you like the subject?
> Does it affect your attitude towards a subject if it is non-examinable? If it does, in what ways?

Each of these is framed like a specific question to a respondent, rather than as an overall research question. None of these could constitute research questions as such, unless there was an adjustment in the wording. The first one might be upgraded to a research question: 'Do examinations make students work harder, make no difference or deter students?' is a researchable question that might make a manageable and interesting thesis or dissertation.

In other cases, there is a mix between research questions and actual interview or questionnaire questions. In the following example, the first question might be framed as the research question, with the others actually being asked as a way of addressing the main question:

> How did English JET (Japanese English Teachers'
> scheme) participants help to internationalize Japanese
> youths?
> What did the experience of being on JET mean to
> them?
> How do they think it contributes to bringing about a
> greater international mindedness and enhanced appre-
> ciation of cultural diversity?

The first question might be better framed in the present
tense – 'How do English JET participants . . .?' – but in
both tenses, a further question goes begging: do we know,
for sure, that Japanese youths *have* been internationalized
by the JET scheme? We would need to know that before
trying to investigate *how* such internationalization has
taken place.

8

Other Ways of Starting Research

Without questions

Some kinds of research do not operate from questions –
at least ostensibly so. Research at the arts and humanities
end of the spectrum in education and social science
research tends to operate neither within the scientific
paradigm nor from the kind of paradigm we have been
assuming throughout most of this book, i.e. a field of
enquiry driven by questions. Rather, it is closer in conven-
tion to the creation of 'monographs' or book-length
works: research that will translate easily into book-form
because it is predicated on that model.

In a Masters thesis on the literary and educational
significance of the Aesopic fable, for example, there is no
question as such. The work progresses from a brief
introduction through chapters on the fable as a genre,
the evolution of the fable, Aesopic fables, moral ideas
about the Aesopic fable, agents in Aesopic fables to a
final one on Aesopic fables as children's literature. The
introduction is contextual and largely historical. It provides both a background and overture to the main body
of the thesis. The final chapter does not so much act as a
conclusion as just another chapter in the design of the
whole – one that gives particular attention to the educational dimension of the research. There is, therefore, a

trajectory and symmetry to the thesis as a whole: through definitions and history, the thesis moves towards its central chapters on the analysis of the Aesopic fable. It ends with the chapter on the fables as children's literature – actual and potential.

Identifying a problem

Many undergraduate degrees in Education and the Social Sciences require students to write a short thesis or dissertation in the final year. Such an assignment can range from 5000 to 15 000 words in length, and is, in effect, like a mini-thesis. It usually contains all the elements of a larger thesis, with a literature review, methodology and empirical dimension. Writing a thesis at this stage is a considerable challenge for undergraduates, as this is often the first occasion on which a work of such scale has been attempted.

This is how one student described the process of working towards a focus for her thesis:

> The initial idea for this dissertation arose out of a recognition (personal, as well as via Nightline [a student counselling service], and through talking generally to fellow students) of the stresses and strains of student life. There seemed to exist, at the time, a 'gap' in the support systems available.

The perception of a 'gap' provides the problem that is to be addressed in the dissertation, *viz* a mismatch between student perceptions of a university counselling service and what the university itself thought it was providing for the students. Indeed, the gradual identification of the problem almost obviated the need for a clear research question. The student used semi-structured interview to elicit perceptions from six fellow-students that would address her aim. The research question is implied: 'What are the perceptions of students in University A of the counselling service in that university?'.

Identifying an area of interest

One of the most interesting theses I have examined was a study of the use of metaphor in education. It had no clearly defined research question, problem or hypothesis. Rather, it simply stated the nature of its interest and proceeded to explore it. The exploration was unconventional, in that there was not the usual definition of the problem, statement of intention, literature review and empirical data-gathering and analysis. Instead, the thesis presented itself as a post-modernist text, with a mix of personal statements, autobiographical writing, conventional critical academic analysis, poetry, blank pages, lists and other types of text. These were not linked together in an explicit way; it was left to the reader to make connections. Thus, although there was an implicit logic in the way the thesis was constructed, it was not spelt out.

The role for the reader/examiner in making sense of such a thesis is a highly proactive one. You have to work harder and think harder than in the reading of a conventional thesis where the explicit connections are made for you. Indeed, in a conventional thesis, it is good advice to make such connections as explicit as possible in order to make the research process transparent to the reader, and to help them navigate through a long (sometimes up to 100 000 words) text. The process of reading with this particular post-modernist text, however, was more inductive.

As there was not a clear starting point of the kind outlined above, it could be said (from a conventional point of view) that the thesis meandered. Such a quality would be damaging to the success of the thesis if conventional criteria were being brought to bear upon it. In the case of the thesis in question, however, there was no need for such a clear starting point as the thesis could actually be read in any sequence.

In the end, the candidate was awarded the PhD with one suggestion for an amendment, *viz* that he or she add a preface to explain to the reader how the thesis should be read. The role of the two external examiners (on that occasion) was to judge what the candidate had produced within the paradigm he or she had chosen. The same criteria applied as for the award of a conventional thesis: these, generally speaking, are that the thesis must make an original contribution to knowledge; it must demonstrate independent critical grasp of a field; it must demonstrate scholarship; and be coherent and well-structured. In terms of its own chosen paradigm, the thesis fulfilled all of these criteria.

Using such an approach to research and the writing of a thesis can be riskier than taking the conventional line. In many ways, the researcher who chooses such an approach must be *more* sure of his or her theoretical basis and methods than someone using the conventional genre.

Compare the success of this particular case with a thesis that was referred and finally failed. Not only did the unsuccessful thesis have no clear starting point, no coherence, no logical or tacit connection between the various chapters, little scholarship and little or no critical dimension; it also had no rationale for its loose and uneven structure. As a piece of research, it would have benefited from a clear starting point in the form of a problem, question or hypothesis from which a methodology could have been generated. This methodology, in turn, would have helped in the eventual structuring of the final thesis.

Via hypotheses

A classic way to start research, especially within a certain, conventional scientific paradigm, is via a hypothesis. In other words, the researcher predicts what he or she thinks might happen under certain conditions and with certain interventions. He or she then sets up a test to prove or disprove the hypothesis. Although *proving* the hypothesis might seem to the most straightforward way to go about testing the hypothesis, it is considered more robust to *disprove* the hypothesis. Any hypothesis could be proved by selecting the right sort of test; but the disproof of a hypothesis gives a clear result, even though it may take more work to be relatively sure that certain factors or variables affect a situation in a particular way.

Cohen *et al.* (2000) discuss hypotheses, referring to the work of Kerlinger (1970) and Medawar (1972, 1981). Hypotheses are statements of 'possible worlds' where relations are posited between two or more factors or variables. They might be the product of an educated guess, but are more likely to emerge from a period of inductive thinking or, dialectically, as an antithesis to some existing 'thesis' or set of ideas and/or assumptions. The hypothesis is then subjected to empirical testing to see if its 'possible world' is anything like the real world. If we are to prove that the hypothesis is 'true', then we must design a study in which the hypothesis is sufficiently precise as to be able to generate or suggest its methods. An elegant and economical design will result in a chance to prove or disprove the hypothesis (both are equally valid outcomes, though the former is likely to have more predictive power).

A study I examined in the mid-1990s approached the effectiveness of a genre-based method in teaching writing in just such a way. Here is how the student set out the method of investigation:

75

The present exploratory study is an attempt to evaluate the effect of one external influence, that is, teaching methodology, and the interaction between that external influence and individual students' cognitive style, on the learning of writing.

That statement might be taken as the *aim* of the study. The hypotheses derive from the aim and emerge as follows:

the writing of nearly all students shows some improvement as a result of genre-based teaching, if the assessment of their performance after the teaching is based on writing completed with access to models and other forms of support;

the improvement produced in student writing as a result of genre-based teaching does not lead to new internalized knowledge;

genre-based teaching will be more effective for students who prefer verbal rather than non-verbal means of representing knowledge.

These three hypotheses were examined by monitoring the change in writing performance by students. The students were asked to write a letter of complaint on a topic of their own choice. They were then taught how to write such a letter using genre-based teaching methods and wrote a second letter. Subsequently, the students were asked to rewrite one of their first letters 'without recourse to the models or other support . . . to establish whether the skills and knowledge they had gained as a result of the genre-based teaching had been internalised' (Howes, 1994, pp. 29–30). There followed further tests, as well as a 'cognitive styles assessment task' to determine whether the students had a preferred means of representing and accessing knowledge.

This is not the place to examine the research instruments in detail; rather, the focus is on how starting a thesis with hypotheses determines the way the research will progress and how it will be reported. The main point to be made is that starting with hypotheses often suggests that the research is attempting to gauge effect or impact. In other words, the research is likely to be operating within a scientific, causal paradigm where it is assumed that x affects y. Effect sizes are often small – which means that a hypothesis will have to be carefully weighted in order to be useful.

Hypotheses are generally thought to be more precise than research questions, in that they may be posed on the basis of a certain degree of knowledge in the field to be explored. Research questions, on the other hand, can be asked on the basis of no prior knowledge. In both cases, precision is important: the sharper the question or hypothesis, the more likely there is to be a clear answer or result.

Furthermore, hypotheses tend to be used within the scientific paradigm, discussed earlier in the book. This is because they operate within the assumption that the truth is discovered via a deductive process or a deductive–inductive oscillation (i.e. between ideas, theories and projections on the one hand, and observation, collected data, empirical testing on the other). In research that emerges from a humanistic or ethnographic paradigm – one that works inductively – hypotheses are likely to be deferred until a certain amount of investigation has taken place. In other words, research in this mode is less likely to start with a hypothesis. The 'hunch' that is often the starting point for research may well take the form of a problem to be solved, or a question to be answered.

One final point: it is more likely that a research question might lead, in due course, to a hypothesis to be tested than it is for the reverse to take place. Such directionality is a result of the fact that research questions tend to be less certain of what kind of result is likely to

77

ensue from the research – and if we expect research to help us to be increasingly clear about a topic, we would expect research questions to help us to formulate hypotheses rather than the other way round.

9

Summary

The following is a summary of stages to go through in creating, refining, applying and answering research questions in your thesis or dissertation.

Finding a topic to research

You should always choose a topic in which you are interested, not one which has been suggested to you by someone else and in which you have only a passing interest. Whether your thesis/dissertation is going to take you six months, a year, three years or even longer, you will need to sustain that interest for the whole period of the research. To put the point more emphatically as far as the topic of the present book goes, you should find a question that you really do want to try to answer: preferably a burning question for you.

The topic or question may emerge from your reading, or from experience, or from an area which you have found has not been covered so far. It may first suggest itself as a rather vague area of interest, but as you follow leads and read more widely, you will find that the picture begins to clear and a question or questions begin to define themselves.

Focusing the topic into a question or questions

The next stage is sharpening your topic into a question or a number of questions. In most cases, these will first emerge as a number of questions. These may or may not hit the target for you very quickly. The most likely scenario is that they will surround the target of the research you want to undertake, approximating your goal to some degree or other.

Your task, therefore, is to consider the various questions you have generated and work out which further questions you might want to consider. It is important to frame these as questions rather than as statements. Once you have a loose collection of questions, try to categorize them into clusters. Which ones go together? Have you got any questions that seem to duplicate other ones (in which case you can eliminate one or two)? Can some questions be dropped?

Identifying the main research question

Identifying the main research question is an important stage in your emerging project. You can do this by arraying the various questions you have generated, and then selecting one as the main, overarching question you are hoping to answer. A simple way to effect this decision is to cut out each question on a separate strip of paper. Move the strips around until you are happy with the relationship between the questions via your arrangement of the strips. You will be able to see which is the outstanding or main question, and whether some of the questions are closely related to it or distantly related. Some of the distant ones you might be able to eliminate.

Once the main research question emerges, you should spend some time refining it, deciding exactly which terms you want in the question. Is this to be a study of the *effect* of one variable on another, or a study of the *nature* or *qualities* of a phenomenon, or a *survey* of attitudes, or some other kind of study? Each word in the research question needs to be given careful consideration, as each word will count in the final reckoning as to whether you have successfully answered the question.

Another important consideration to bear is mind is whether the research question is *answerable* within the time-scale and resources you have at your disposal.

Working out the subsidiary questions (if any)

What happens to the other questions you generated? Are they to be retained as subsidiary questions, or dropped from the research design entirely?

Once you have decided that, you can determine what kind of subsidiary questions you have. Are they contributory, in that answering them will contribute to the answer of your overall main question, or are they ancillary in that they follow from or emerge from an attempt to answer the main question? This is an important distinction, because it has implications for how the answers will be reported.

Furthermore, how do the various subsidiary questions relate to each other and to the main question? If there is a clear connection to the main question, the relationship of the subsidiary questions to each other should be easier to work out. But there will still need to be some consideration of the relative position of the subsidiary questions: are they clustered into sub-topics? Do they have a logical relation to each other? Are some more important than others?

81

How does the main question determine the choice of research methods?

When the main research question and any subsidiary questions have been established, part of the methodology has been fixed. Is it then possible to choose which research methods will be best suited to answering the main research question.

Questions which include the term 'effect' are likely to require a randomized controlled trial, as this is generally accepted to be the best method for measuring the effect of an intervention. Questions which address 'impact' or 'influence' are likely to wish to consider a number of factors and thus will not want to control factors or variables as tightly as controlled trials, with their experimental and control groups. Questions about attitudes or those which try to determine the nature of a case – like case studies – will want to use attitude scales and a range of research methods, some of which will lead to qualitative outcomes, respectively. Some questions will require a purely qualitative approach.

Part of the supervision and examination of a thesis/ dissertation it to see how well the intended question or questions fits the methods used to answer it or them.

Where do the questions appear in the thesis/ dissertation?

Because research questions are key structural devices in the conduct of a research project, they need to figure prominently in the write-up of the thesis or dissertation. It is common for them to appear during the introduction, followed by a brief rationale as to why they are important (for example, how they help to answer a problem), and how they inform the methodology and methods used. Furthermore, an introduction usually sets out what the following chapters of the thesis/dissertation are, and how each of them contributes to the answering of the research question.

Research questions may also appear at the beginning of the empirical part of a thesis or dissertation, for example at the beginning of the methodology chapter, at the beginning of the results chapter(s) and again in the conclusion.

They may emerge from a literature review and appear at the end of that review, to indicate that the formulation of the question has been complex and has derived from existing literature in the field.

How are questions answered?

At some point in the thesis, the research question and any subsidiary questions have to be answered. Although some researchers include rhetorical questions in their text, it is always a risky approach because if a question is raised in research (unless it is a question arising from the research and set out as worthy of further research or inquiry) there should be an attempt to answer it. The notion of the 'answerable' question is thus a common one in research, even if that means that some of the more interesting questions, which are not readily answerable, go unasked.

Answers to research questions can appear either in the discussion section of a results chapter or chapters, in a separate discussion chapter, and/or in the conclusion. Any question that is formally presented in the first part of the thesis or dissertation must be answered.

If there are contributory questions to the overarching

main question, these should be answered first; if, on the other hand, the subsidiary questions are ancillary to the main question, they can be answered after the main question is addressed.

References and Further Reading

Al-Suwaidi, A. A. (2001) *The Assessment of Comprehension Skills and Development of a Programme for Enhancing Comprehension Skills for Fourth Grade Students in the State of Qatar,* unpublished PhD thesis, University of Hull.

Andrews, R. (1992) *An Exploration of Structural Relationships in Narrative and Argumentative Writing, with Particular Reference to the Work of Year 8 Students,* unpublished PhD thesis, University of Hull.

Bell, J. (1999) *Doing Your Research Project,* Buckingham: Open University Press.

Cao, N. (2002) *The Status of Music in the Primary School Curriculum,* unpublished MA thesis, University of York.

Campbell, A., Philips, S. and Gilroy, P. (2002) *Research for Professional Development,* London: Paul Chapman.

Cohen, L., Manion, L and Morrison, K. (2000) *Research Methods in Education,* London: RoutledgeFalmer (5th edn).

Dean, A. (1995) *Perceptions of a Counselling Service in Relation to the Reality/Experience of Student Life: Six Students at University A,* Middlesex University, BA in Education Studies, proposition module.

Department for Education and Employment/ Qualifications and Curriculum Authority (1999) *The National Curriculum for England,* London: Her Majesty's Stationery Office.

De Vaus, D. (2001) *Research Design in Social Research*, London: Sage.

Denscombe, M. (2002) *Ground Rules for Good Research*, Buckingham: Open University Press.

Featherstone, V. (1997) *Mature Women Students: Experiences and Strategies – A Small Local Study*, unpublished MA dissertation, University of Hull.

Gan, L. (2002) *Chinese Students' Perceptions of English Teaching and Learning in China*, unpublished MA thesis, University of York.

Gorard, S. (2001) *Quantitative Methods in Educational Research*, London: Continuum.

Howes, D. (1994) *A Study into the Effectiveness of a Genre-Based Approach to Teaching Writing*, a minor thesis submitted in partial fulfilment of the requirements for the degree of Master of Education at The University of Melbourne.

Hui, W. (2002) *Should Putonghua be a Medium of Instruction in Hong Kong Schools?*, Unpublished MA thesis, University of York.

Kerlinger, F. N. (1970) *Foundations of Behavioral Research*, New York: Holt, Reinhart and Winston.

Kwok, Kam Fun (2001) *Learning to Write in English in Hong Kong: An Exploration of Syntactic and Textual Aspects of Writing by Children in a Hong Kong Primary School*, unpublished PhD thesis, University of London, Institute of Education.

Lee, J. (2002) *The Educational and Cultural Impact of the 1998 Medium of Instruction Policy on Secondary Education in Hong Kong*, unpublished PhD thesis, University of York.

Levinovic-Healy, A. H. (1999) *Children Reading in a Post-typographic Age: Two Case Studies*, unpublished PhD, Queensland University of Technology.

Litosseliti, L. (2003) *Focus Groups*, London: Continuum.

Medawar, P. (1972) *The Hope of Progress*, London: Methuen.

Medawar, P. (1981) *Advice to a Young Scientist*, London: Pan.

Mitchell, S. (1992) *Questions and Schooling*, Hull: University of Hull, School of Education, Centre for Studies in Rhetoric (Occasional Research Papers no. 1), reprinted in Andrews, R. and Mitchell, S. (2001) *Essays in Argument*, London: Middlesex University Press.

Oakley, A. (2001) *Experiments in Knowing*, Cambridge: Polity Press.

Pérez, T. (2003) *The Use of Web-Based Self-Access Language Learning Material in a Higher Education Language Centre*, unpublished material submitted for upgrading from MPhil to PhD, University of York.

Puri, E. (2002) *Investigating the Perceptions of Student Teachers Involved in the EC-Canadian 'Promoting Citizenship Education through Initial Teacher Education' Project*, unpublished MA thesis, University of York.

Scott, D. and Usher, R. (1999) *Researching Education: Data, Methods and Theory in Educational Enquiry*, London: Cassell.

Sharma, C. B. (1994) *Multimedia Approaches to Teaching Literature: A Study of the Use of Hypermedia in the Teaching of English as a Non-native Literature in a Number of Indian Universities*, unpublished PhD thesis, University of Hull.

Tabor, D. (2001) *Writing Demands Across the Transition from Primary to Secondary School: A Case Study*, unpublished PhD thesis, University of Warwick.

Toulmin, S. (1958) *The Uses of Argument*, Cambridge: Cambridge University Press.

Tsaliki, E. (2002) *Perceptions, Processes and Experiences of the Teaching of English as Second Language*, unpublished MA thesis, University of York.

Walford, G. (2001) *Doing Qualitative Educational Research*, London: Continuum.

Wellington, J. (2000) *Educational Research*, London: Continuum.

Yang, Q. (2002) *Examinations: Friend or Foe? Students' Perceptions of the Role of Examinations in Students' Life: a Comparison between British and Chinese Students*, unpublished MA thesis, University of York.

Yannicopoulou, A. (1989) *An Examination of the Literary and Educational Significance of the Aesopic Fable*, unpublished MEd thesis, University of Hull.

You, J. (2002) *Factors Helping High School Students in China to Develop English Conversational Skills*, unpublished MA thesis, University of York.

Index